The Theory Of Bellytivity

by

J.M.O'Belly

MENU: The Breakfast, Lunch, and Dinner Table of Contents

MENU: THE BREAKFAST, LUNCH, AND DINNER TABLE OF CONTENTS   3

FOREWORD: FOUR WORDS / FOREWARNING   9

INTRODUCTION: I FEEL YOUR GAIN   11

CHAPTER 1. HEAVY MATH   15

The Theory Of Bellytivity   17

Basic Is Beautiful   19

The State Of Ideal Weight   21

The Zen Of When   23

Geometry For Tummies   25

CHAPTER 2. SIX WEIGHTED QUESTIONS   27

Who?   29

What?   31

When?   33

Where?   35

Why?   37

hoW?   39

Questioning The Answers   41

CHAPTER 3. THE BIG PICTURE   43

Genes 'R' Us   45

Long, Long Ago   47

Whatever Whenever   49

Let Them Eat Cake   51

Make Them Eat Cake   53

Bring It On Home   55

The Industrial Waistline   57

The United States Of Advertising   59

CHAPTER 4. GO, FIGURE   61

Belly Is As Belly Does   63

Living Life Large   65

Idle Momentum   67

Virtual Obesity   69

Concession Confession   71

Grazing Gain   73

ChemiCalories   75

The Weak End   77

Lookin' For Lunch In All The Wrong Places   79

Late Weight   81

Me, Myself, And Ice Cream   83

CHAPTER 5. WEIGHING IN   85

A Balancing Act   87

It's About Time   89

The Joy Of Being Cooked For   91

Braving The Craving   93

Just Don't Do It   95

Exorcise Those Pounds Away   97

Running Lapses   99

CHAPTER 6. ZEN AND THE ART OF METABOLIC MAINTENANCE   101

Stream Of Unconsciousness   103

Belly And The Beast   105

Where There's A Weigh There's A Will   107

Lighten Up!   109

To Market, To Market   111

EPILOGUE: AFTER WORDS   113

Words To Live And Diet By   115

GLOSSARY   117

FOREWORD: Four Words / Forewarning

FOUR WORDS: Breakfast   Lunch   Dinner   Water.

FOREWARNING: Four more words - **Not For Every Body.** This book contains educational information, not medical advice, and is not intended to replace the medical advice of your doctor and/or health care provider.

Hey, Don't Start This "diet" Unless You've Seen Your Doctor, Been Checked Out, And Told That It's O.K. to try it.

Why? Because your Doctor and/or Health Care Provider can determine if you are healthy enough and ready to avoid calories between meals (i.e. to eat Three Square Meals A Day and consume Only Water between meals – the concept of this "diet").

Think Smart: Tell your Doctor if you've never gone without calories between meals; or, if you think you've ever had any trouble going without calories between meals; or, if you think you might have trouble if you were to go without calories between meals; or, if you have excessive thirst, excessive urination, or dehydration; or, if you have, or think you might have, a past history or a family history of Diabetes Mellitus, Metabolic Syndrome, Pre-Diabetes, Hypoglycemia ("Low Blood Sugar"), Diabetes Insipidus, Cardiac Arrhythmia, Kidney or Liver Disease, or any condition affected by diet or requiring a special diet; or, if you take any medications, herbs, supplements, etc.; or, if you've been told that you're "too thin" or that you don't need to lose weight; or, if you are under 18 years of age; or, if you're obese or even just overweight. Again, don't start this "diet" unless you've seen your Doctor, been checked out, and told it's o.k. to try it.

Once you've been given the O.K. to start this plan, keep people and caloric food and/or drink around you at first – just in case. If you don't feel right when you try this "diet" (e.g. sweating, shakiness, lightheadedness, confusion, headache, other), stop and seek medical treatment immediately.
Ready?   O.K   Here we go!

[pause]

INTRODUCTION: I Feel Your Gain

One day, after doing the math, I figured that the odds of my becoming a lottery winner were diminishing, ticket-by-ticket.

So, I decided it was About Time to do the next best thing – to write a "diet" book. Why not?

After exhaustively researching the subject (Weight, Gravity, Momentum, Energy, Time, Human Nature, Other), I think that, amazingly, I may have discovered the Problem:

There's something Bigger here than just our Bellies.

We're slowly being stripped (not a very pretty picture for some of us) of: our Dignity, our Pride, our Independence, our Individuality, our Self-Esteem, and our Self-Reliance. Ouch!!

Other than that, "Not a Problem."

O.K. We already know <u>What</u> To Eat – proteins, fats, and carbohydrates – and we have a good idea of how our food should be proportioned and prepared, so that it's Healthy. We just need to remember <u>When</u>, And <u>When</u> <u>Not</u>, To Eat.

Hey, I'm saying: <u>Put</u> <u>A</u> <u>Clock</u> <u>On</u> <u>It</u> - not an "Open 24/7" sign.

So, what's the point? The point is this:

We don't need Cheerleaders, Drill Sergeants, or Con Artists telling us what to do. We can Make Our Own Decisions.
We want it SIMPLE. We want it DO-ABLE.
We Need BELLYTIVITY; We Need It Bad; We Need It Now.

[pause]

Well, Here It Is!

For the first 2 weeks: $3^2 + H_2O$.
You'll try to eat 3 Square Meals A Day.
You'll try to allow no more than 1 hour for each meal.
You'll try to consume Only Water between meals.
You'll try to record daily weights and notes about any lapses.

For awhile after that: Lifestyle meets Bellytivity.
You'll utilize Your brain to fit the plan into Your lifestyle; then,
You'll adjust Your lifestyle symbiotically (wow!) to fit the plan.

Finally: The Zen of When.
You'll just weigh every day, continuing basically $3^2 + H_2O$.
You'll adjust your intake as needed to keep a healthy weight.

O.K. Now, so Why Read The Book?   Good Question.
It'll strengthen your awareness of the "environment" around
you, the expected and unexpected "temptations" out there;
and it'll remind you of the need to Make Your Own Decisions
and to Stick With Them. After finishing this book, you'll be
able to:

SMILE
When You Say
"NO, THANK YOU."

Hey, It's Your Choice.   So, Help Yourself!

[pause]

Chapter 1. HEAVY MATH

mathematicians
boot camp
geophysical landmass
an inner voice
a boat

IN THE END, IT ALL ADDS UP

In 1684, Newton's Theory of Universal Gravitation ($F_g = G \times m_1m_2/r^2$) was dropped upon us.

In 1905, in zoomed Einstein's Theory of Relativity ($E = mc^2$).

Don't get me wrong, now; these were two Huge theories, by two Heavy Hitters.

Problem is that Isaac appeared to be more focused on Gravity than on Weight and Al just seemed to make Light of the subject.

Neither addressed the Gravity Of Weight that we see and feel around us today.

The Theory of Bellytivity ($E = 3^2 + H_2O$) at last has arrived and, hey, It's about Time!

[pause]

The Theory Of Bellytivity

"Since the mathematicians have invaded the theory of relativity, I do not understand it myself anymore."
Albert Einstein (1879 – 1955).

So, I'm at the old blackboard one morning working on the Theory of Square Progression: $x^2 = (x - 1)^2 + 2x - 1$.

Just as I plug 3 into the formula, my stomach growls and I think about Lunch – one of my 3 square meals.

Suddenly, it dawns on me (not quite a Eureka Moment or an Apple Dropping Moment, but still a Moment) that the plan I had been using for many years for (mostly) healthy eating can be "reduced" to a simple formula:

The energy needed (E) by a healthy individual to achieve and maintain a healthy weight and lifestyle can be obtained from 3 square meals per day (3^2) plus water (H_2O). So,

$$E = 3^2 + H_2O$$

becomes a formula for Healthy Eating and

THE THEORY OF BELLYTIVITY

is discovered and named.

(Hey, I had to call it something!)

[pause]

Basic Is Beautiful

"Moderation, the noblest gift of Heaven."
Euripides (484 – 406 B.C.)

$3^2 + H_2O$.

Three Square Meals per day.
Nothing between meals but Water.

That's All, Folks!

A couple of weeks after starting this routine, your stomach will appear to have "shrunk" and you probably won't want quite as much food at each meal. This Is Good!

Bellytivity is simply the Responsible Awareness of <u>When</u> (<u>and</u> <u>When</u> <u>Not</u>) to put calories into One's Own Stomach.

WHY NOT
NOT?

Picture you and your stomach away at boot camp for 2 weeks of Basic Training.
Part of the training involves eating 3 square meals a day.
Between meals, you're kept busy doing things.
You don't have time, nor are you allowed, to stop and snack.
Believe it or not, you can get your stomach "into shape" by practicing $3^2 + H_2O$ every day.

[pause]

The State Of Ideal Weight

Alaska is the heaviest state. Rhode Island is the lightest.
(We're talking Geophysical Landmass here.)

None of us came into the world with a tag attached saying:
"Maximum Occupancy 120 (or 240, or 360, or ___) Pounds.

What's a healthy weight for you? Don't know?
Who can you ask? Right! Your Doctor!

Borrowing from the field of Historical Futurism, we can apply
both The Hundred Year Rule and The Ten Year Rule:

In 100 years, how much difference will it make to you how
much you weighed this year? Probably not much.

In 10 (20? 30?) years, how much difference will it make to
you how much you weighed this year? Possibly quite a bit.

Shall we proceed?

GO, FIGURE.

Picture yourself learning your ideal weight - think of it as your
"destination." All you need to do is get behind the wheel and drive
yourself over a few bumps and turns in the road all the way to that
healthy weight and, once you get to where you want to be, just
continue living in the beautiful State Of Ideal Weight!

[pause]

The Zen Of When

"Don't let the noise of others' opinions drown out your own inner voice."
Steve Jobs (1955 – 2011).

Mind Over Matter matters. It comes into play when Hunger pangs you and reMinds you to think about your next meal.

When Hunger happens, it's often way easier to just grab and down a snack or beverage of some sort, rather than to wait until mealtime.

Remember that Bellytivity involves Responsible Awareness. You need to be constantly on the lookout for Obesetacles. These are situations, habits, circumstances, and conditions that can potentially get in your way as you try to avoid the temptation of Peripheral Calories (calories not obtained during your 3 square meals per day).

ThinK.

Picture yourself driving past one-after-another of those all too familiar, often very colorful, Fast-Food-Forks-In-The-Road.
You might be getting a little hungry now, but you think to yourself:
"Hey, I'm between meals here" and you just keep going.
Your Mind stays on your driving – which is what Matters.

[pause]

Geometry For Tummies

At the base of every food pyramid lies a square.
(Did I say that?)

Tired of all those triangles, "food" wheels, "pie" charts, and endless pyramids? Me too.

Here are the 3 "Food Groups" I try to remember:

Breakfast
Lunch
Dinner

(The Three Squares)

THINK
INSIDE
THE BOXES.

Picture yourself on a boat for an entire day, with nothing on board to eat or drink except water.
Now, picture 3 square boxes (O.K., cubes if you will) – yellow, green, red – tied to the boat and floating on a sea of bright blue water.
Each box contains a Healthy, Square Meal.
Each box lid has a lock with a timer on it.
One timer is set for your breakfast hour, one for your lunch hour, and one for your dinner hour.
I think you can handle it from here!

[pause]

Chapter 2. SIX WEIGHTED QUESTIONS

suspects
sour milk
a smart phone
Voltaire
Superman
attempts
reason

LET'S GET TO THE BOTTOM OF THIS

Who?
What?
When?
Where?
Why?
hoW?

(The 6 W's)

[pause]

Who?

When you consume calories anytime outside the breakfast, lunch, and dinner hours, you're taking in Peripheral Calories.

The act of consuming Peripheral Calories is called a Lapse.

Who might be involved in your Peripheral Calorie Lapses?

I can think of one person.

Anybody else come to mind?

THE
USUAL
SUSPECTS.

Picture yourself as, say, the President of the United States (why not?).
You have surrounded yourself with advisors.
Half of your advisors are telling you to go ahead and eat the Donut; the other half remind you what the White House Chef has on the menu for your upcoming Meal.
What're you going to do?   It's <u>Your</u> Choice.

[*pause*]

What?

"One swears by wholemeal bread alone, one by sour milk; vegetarianism is the only road to salvation for some, others insist not only on vegetables alone, but on eating those raw. At one time, the only thing that matters is calories; at another time, they are crazy about vitamins or about roughage.
"The scientific truth may be put quite briefly; eat moderately, having an ordinary mixed diet, and don't worry."
Sir Robert Hutchison (1871 – 1960), *Newcastle Medical Journal*, Vol. 12, 1932.

What are you putting into that stomach between meals?

_____Fast food.   _____Snacks.
_____"Energy" food or drink.   _____Hot drinks.
_____Cold drinks.   _____Soft drinks.
_____Hard drinks.   _____Beer.
_____Wine.   _____Candy.
_____"Sugar free" food or drink.   _____"Lite" food or drink.
_____"Low fat" food or drink.   _____"Diet" food or drink.
_____Other.

What do you eat for Breakfast? Lunch? Dinner?

_____Healthy Food.   _____Unhealthy Food.

GOT WATER?

Picture yourself sitting in a lecture by Sir Robert (see quote above), trying to stay awake. When he tells you to: "eat moderately, having an ordinary mixed diet, and don't worry," doesn't it kinda remindya of the book you're reading? Eat three square meals a day; eat healthy food; consume only water between meals; and Lighten Up!

[pause]

When?

"A man seldom thinks with more earnestness of anything than he does of his dinner."
Sam Johnson (1709 – 1784).

When do you eat?

_____Scheduled meals.   _____Whenever it's convenient.
_____Between meals.   _____"What meals?"
_____Late at night.   _____All of the above.
_____Other.

When you get hungry between meals, what do you do?

_____Eat a snack or candy.   _____Drink a soft drink.
_____Drink some water.
_____Other.

It's a
KNOW WHEN
Situation.

Picture Sam (see quote above) looking at his smart phone to see how long until dinner; then taking a couple of sips of water; then calling home to ask what's cookin'.
Maybe that's why they call it a "smart phone."

[pause]

Where?

"Build it and they will come."
Attributed to many, including:
Voltaire (1694 – 1778) and Ronald McDonald (1963 -   ).

Where do you eat (or drink) Peripheral Calories?

_____At fast food restaurants.   _____At parties.
_____At slow food restaurants.   _____In cars.
_____In front of vending machines.   _____In bars.
_____In a closet.   _____At ballgames.
_____In your bedroom.   _____At the movies.
_____In front of a television set.   _____At meetings.
_____At work.   _____At school.
_____In front of a desktop, laptop, tablet, or smartphone.
_____Other.

BEEN HERE,
DONE THIS.

Try to picture some of those places where you've found yourself eating (or drinking) between meals.
Now, which one(s) contributed the most Peripheral Calories?

[pause]

Why?

"There is no sincerer love than the love of food."
George Bernard Shaw (1856 – 1950), *Man and Superman*.

Why do you consume calories between meals?

_____You don't (it's just "slow metabolism").
_____Subconscious (you just find yourself eating).
_____Hunger/appetite (you're just answering the signal).
_____Others are doing it.
_____It was there (like the mountaineer and the mountain).
_____Lack of discipline.
_____Skipped a meal.
_____All of the above.
_____Other.

WHY
WEIGHT?

Picture yourself between meals, holding a snack or beverage, just about to put it to your mouth.
Then notice the hesitation on your part, as you ask yourself "Why?"
Then see yourself taking a couple of sips of water instead.
Congratulations, you avoided a potential Lapse!
Chalk one up for Bellytivity!

[pause]

hoW?

"Be Prepared."
Robert Baden-Powell (1857 – 1941).

How do you eat?

_____With family at scheduled meals.
_____With friends at scheduled meals.
_____With others at scheduled meals.
_____Alone at scheduled meals.
_____In front of a television or other screen.
_____Quickly.
_____Slowly.
_____Grazingly.
_____Haphazardly.
_____Snackingly.
_____Other.

HOW DO YOU DON'T?

Picture one of your recent attempts at having a meal. Was there much planning or preparation involved? Now picture your next 3 meals. How much planning has gone into them? How much snacking is likely to go on between those meals?

[pause]

Questioning The Answers

The 6 W's might bring to light obvious behavior patterns; or there may be more subtle clues: people, foods, times of day, locations, excuses, schedules, other.

You might even want to ask yourself, again, if $3^2 + H_2O$ is right for You.

It's ALIMENTARY, My Dear Watson.

Picture visiting your Doc, making sure it will be safe for you to skip calories between meals; then, picture yourself lapsing on your way home.
Wow, that was quick! What happened?
wwwwwwhatcha gonna do now?

[pause]

Chapter 3. THE BIG PICTURE

DNA
yabba dabba
an oyster
be merry
number$
good lookin'
a model t
someone else

IT'S BIGGER THAN THE BOTH OF US

About 4,700,000,000 years ago (give or take a few years), scientists think the Earth was formed.
It's been aRound for quite awhile, now.
Gravity came with the package.
Since weight = mass x gravity, Weight showed up right about that very same time.
Weight has been out there, just hanging around, ever since.

About 3,700,000,000 years ago, scientists think the first cellular organism may have appeared.
I would imagine it woke up hungry.
Hunger has been out there, just panging away, ever since.

Maybe about 0,000,195,000 years ago, scientists think Homo sapiens finally arrived - hungry as expected.
Human Beings have been out there, just Being Human, ever since.

[pause]

Genes 'R' Us

"It is in our genes to understand the universe if we can, to keep trying even if we cannot, and to be enchanted by the act of learning all the way."
Lewis Thomas (1913 – 1993).

The drives (or instincts) to Hunt, Gather, Eat, Store, etc. are engraved into our DNA.

They are there to help the human, as well as other, species to survive – and we have!

Just as a bird migrates every autumn and spring, or a salmon swims from the ocean back up the river of its birth to mate and die, we have a very strong instinct to Eat, in order not to perish.

SURVIVAL
OF
THE
FATTEST?

When our very early ancestors got hungry, there wasn't a refrigerator in the kitchen, or a kitchen in the house, or even a little house somewhere out there on the prairie.
Those who "stored" the most each time they ate may have had a survival advantage over those who didn't. Picture that.

[pause]

Long, Long Ago

"Here's some advice. Stay alive."
Susan Collins (1962 -   ), *The Hunger Games*.

Our ancestors were reminded frequently not to miss the next opportunity to Calorize.

In our one-on-every-corner "environment," however, there are so many "next opportunities" waving and shouting at us everywhere we go, all the time, in exchange for the expenditure of almost no energy, that we have a different problem:
Saying "No, Thank You."

YABBA
DABBA
DON'T!

Picture yourself chasing animals, building fires, digging roots, picking berries – alongside your long ago ancestors in their struggle to survive. Are you starting to get a little hungry just thinking about it? Now, picture yourself between square meals, walking or driving past a donut shop or fast food place, trying not to "seize" the "opportunity."

[pause]

Whatever Whenever

"He was a bold man that first ate an oyster."
Jonathan Swift (1667 – 1745).

Those way back relatives did a lot of wandering in search of food – just to stay alive.

They ate some "interesting" stuff along the way before "eliminating" the bad and "retaining" the good for future reference.

Fortunately, the valuable knowledge of which foods are "safe" for us and which are not was passed along to us by some very brave ancestors.

THEY TOOK WHAT THEY GOT.
THEY GOT WHAT THEY TOOK.

Picture yourself as part of a hungry group of wandering humans thousands of years ago encountering an unknown plant, or animal, or stream, for the first time. Then, suddenly, everyone points at you to remind you that it's your turn to be the brave one!

[pause]

Let Them Eat Cake

"Live simply so others may simply live."
Mother Teresa (1910 – 1997).

Fast forward to medieval times.

Some of those surviving nomadic ancestors found themselves part of a country (kingdom, fiefdom, empire – whatever you might want to call it).

When not at war, and with little to do besides count money, one of the "nobility" may have invented the Snack.

The "nobility" soon realized that they were able to eat whenever they were hungry.

This meant that the people who sat atop the pyramid often became the heaviest (not a pretty picture).

EAT, DRINK, AND BE MERRY (FOR ABOUT AN HOUR).

Picture K, Q, & J peering out the window of the castle while snacking, making certain that the workers in the fields weren't slacking.

[pause]

Make Them Eat Cake

"Would yee both eat your cake and have your cake?"
John Heywood (1497 – 1580); *Proverbes, Part II, Chap. IX.*

Later on, after a few heads rolled and the economic picture improved, the first of many Caloric Entrepreneurs arrived on the scene, accompanied by a team of Sales Pitchers.

"Let's Make Every Body <u>Want</u> To Eat Cake All Day Long!

"Sure, the King, Queen, and Jack are already snacking, but what about all those <u>Number$</u> out there? As long as they have money to spend on snacks and drinks, We Can Help!"

SNACK
DAB
IN THE
MIDDLE.

Picture buying a snack and eating it between meals.
Picture buying a beverage and drinking it between meals.
Picture skipping the snack and beverage and waiting until mealtime.

[pause]

Bring It On Home

"Hey, good lookin', whacha got cookin'?"
Hank Williams (1923 – 1953).

Some of our forebears landed and stayed in the city; many others wound up, for one reason or another, in some pretty remote zip codes, where they awoke each morning with domesticated animals and planted vegetables not far away.

They all still had that hunger drive (just as we have today), but, out of necessity, they developed a Schedule:

Breakfast
Work
Lunch
Work
Dinner
Sleep.

So, between meals, they were either working (hard, physical, calorie-burning work for most) or sleeping. If they got a little hungry or thirsty between meals, they brought along Water – not flavored or sweetened beverages – just Water.

WATER
WORKS.

Let's see…no snacks; hard, physical, calorie-burning work…hmmm.

[pause]

The Industrial Waistline

In 1913, Henry Ford began building the Model T on a moving assembly line, which helped to lower the cost of a Model T and, at the same time, to raise workers' wages. The workers moved less, thus increasing Industrial Efficiency.

The development of machinery to do more and more of the physical work led to workers expending fewer and fewer calories.

The calories were burned in factories and vehicles and were expelled through smokestacks and exhaust pipes, instead of sweat glands.

CAUTION:
WIDE
LOAD.

Picture the workers continuing to eat more often: more choices available, more convenience, more breaks, more wages - but fewer calories burned. Now, picture the waistlines expanding to equal, or even exceed, those of the bosses, many of whom had already ballooned.

[pause]

The United States Of Advertising

"Be yourself –
not your idea of what you think someone else's idea of yourself should be."
Henry David Thoreau (1817 – 1862).

In the mid 19th century, there was the Mail Order Catalogue.

Then, over the decades, came Newspaper, Magazine, and Radio ads.

Television arrived: the first commercial T.V. ad aired in 1941.

Then came Cable (which began without ads).

The Internet came along, started so that governments, organizations, and educational institutions could share information.

In came the Dot Coms (1985), then Social Media and Dot Everything. Once again, they're trying to Make Us Want:

WHATEVER
THEY WANT US
TO WANT.

Picture a snack, beverage, or fast food ad: those beautiful, very Trim people, eating and drinking; the pleasant surroundings; the familiar music; the smiles.
The ad stimulates your appetite, which makes you assume you're hungry, which makes you want to take between-meal action.
But you don't, because you're using Bellytivity!

[pause]

Chapter 4. GO, FIGURE

rocket science
bears
Newton
the program
fingers and toes
four stomachs
tinkering
Pavlov
cookery
an enchilada
soul-stirring

WEIGHT HAPPENS

For the past few decades, scientists have become aware of an increase in the weight and girth of the U.S. population.

I guess scientists walk around looking at people, too, just like the rest of us.

[*pause*]

Belly Is As Belly Does

"Nothing makes a woman more beautiful than the belief that she is beautiful."
Sophia Loren (1934 -   ).

"Why me?" Why so much me?" "Why can't I...?" you ask.

Because you've put more calories into your body than you've burned.

It's not Rocket Science.

Speaking of rocket science, do you think the rocket scientist, or the brain surgeon, got there without study and discipline?

Did the athlete, or the musician, get there without practice and discipline?

Did I just say "discipline" twice?

Just
DON'T
Do It.

Try to picture the last time you remember <u>turning down</u> the offer of food or beverage between meals.
Way to go!   Bellytivity! $3^2 + H_2O$!
Now, try to continue to practice smiling as you say: "No, Thank You."

[pause]

Living Life Large

"Vision is the art of seeing things invisible."
Jonathan Swift (1667 – 1745).

It's obvious that excess weight eventually leads to excess wear and tear on one's body: most noticeably on muscles, joints, ligaments, tendons, cartilage, and blood vessels.

That "bears" repeating; so, here it is again, in a step-by-step format:

A lot of extra weight
       for a long period of time
              can damage the body
                     in many ways.

IT'S
YOUR
CHOICE.

Picture carrying around two 10 (or 5, or 2) pound bags of potatoes, or sand, or dog food, or something. Then imagine putting one bag down, but continuing to carry the other bag. Immediately, you notice less effort needed to carry just one bag. However, as you continue carrying the one bag, you notice the extra weight you're still carrying and, when you put that bag down, it's yet a little easier for you to get around and about. How about that!

[pause]

Idle Momentum

The first television remote control (named "Lazy Bones") was created in 1950.

Momentum = mass x velocity.

It's commonly confused with Newton's First Law of Motion:
Bodies at rest tend to stay at rest;
Bodies in motion tend to stay in motion.

Well, anyway, try to follow:

The longer a body sits still on a couch, the harder it is for that body to get up off the couch.

If we add to that the Passive Activity involved in motionlessly staring at a screen, watching activities performed by others, burning almost no calories, we've got Idle Momentum – bigtime!

IDLE.
IDLE MOMENT.
IDLE MOMENTUM.
IDLE MOMENTUMMY.

Picture yourself sprawled out on a couch with your "Lazy Bones" (see above) clicking away, effortlessly moving from channel to channel – an ideal setting for the development of Virtual Obesity (next page).

[pause]

Virtual Obesity

"The more elaborate our means of communication, the less we communicate."
Joseph Priestley (1733 – 1804).

This is a "no-brainer" (so is television, come to think of it).

Virtual Obesity is a consequence of Passive Activity.

Virtually all those scientists out there tend to agree that increased television viewing (or viewing almost any screen, for that matter) is associated with an increase in weight.

So, if you're trying to lose weight, then, seems to me, there's not much room for television in the "program."

T.V. OR NOT T.V.?
FAT IS THE QUESTION.

Why do we watch it?
Good question.
Why do we eat more than we should?
Good question.
Who, What, When, Where, Why, hoW?
Good questions.

[pause]

Concession Confession

"What we play is life."
Louis Armstrong (1901 - 1971).

I confess that I spent many years (and many, many dollars) buying popcorn at movie concession stands. No regrets.

Concession is a very interesting word. It means "a Yielding."

The concession stands at movie theaters have a lot in common with those at ballgames and concerts and, in fact, with vending machines and even with that kitchen around the corner from the old couch:

They all are Purveyors of Peripheral Calories; and they are located "conveniently" wherever and whenever we are ready to Yield to the "suggestion" that we "need" to eat or drink.

As the caloric entrepreneurs and their loyal sales pitchers would put it, "We're here to help!"

You might want to give a little forethought as to how "fully" you'll partake of those easily accessible peripheral calories you'll encounter at those enjoyable experiences you've chosen to experience and enjoy. It's Your Choice.

PLAY IT AGAIN, SLIM.

Picture yourself "at the pictures." Count the number of "suggestions" you receive, from the time the ticket taker takes your ticket to the time the feature actually starts. Got enough fingers and toes?

[*pause*]

Grazing Gain

Some scientists say that a cow has four stomachs. Others argue that it's one stomach with four separate compartments - whatever. If one adds to that the capacity (60 gallons), then it's a pretty good excuse for eating all the time.

Eating whenever you want to (or even when you don't particularly want to) is not a whole lot different from what cattle do all day long.

They're allowed to do so in order for them to gain as much weight as possible so as to be sold by the pound for slaughter.

Before slaughter, however, most cattle are put into a confined space, with already-prepared food (fast food?) in front of them, and nothing to do but eat.

That's when they go from overweight to obese.

The
WEIGHTING
Game.

Picture a row of cattle munching away at a trough full of feed.
Now, picture yourself walking into an all-night-all-you-can-eat buffet.
Let's see: bellytivity...responsible awareness...when and when not....

[pause]

ChemiCalories

In 1957, Glucose Isomerase was discovered, making it possible to convert the glucose in corn syrup into fructose, resulting in High Fructose Corn Syrup.

I try to watch out for substitutes.

ChemiCalories are calories derived from molecules that have been "tinkered with."
Whenever "they" decide to substitute ChemiCalories for natural calories, I tend to wonder: "What're they up to <u>now</u>?"

Examples of ChemiCalories include: Partially Hydrogenated Vegetable Oils, Trans-Fatty Acids, and High Fructose Corn Syrup.

A cousin of the ChemiCalorie is the PseudoCalorie (alias "Phantom Calorie") – a chemical that tastes like a calorie, but isn't a calorie.

Artificial Sweeteners are examples of PseudoCalories.

Sometimes,
It's Not Nice To
"Fool With"
Mother Nature.

Try to think back and picture various products (not just food and drink) that went through "new and improved" phases. In many cases, the only thing that "improved" was the company's bottom line.

[pause]

The Weak End

The brain is there to think, we think. Our brains think subconsciously, as well as consciously. The brain picks up signals from the five senses (sight, hearing, touch, smell, and taste) and messages from the more subconscious drives (hunger, thirst, fear, pleasure, other).

Unless we can block the subconscious response to a suggestion of hunger, we come running when Dr. Pavlov rings his bell…and bells are ringing almost everywhere, almost all the time.

NO BRAIN,
NO LOSS.

Try to picture the gas gauge on a car. Imagine what it would be like if it were calibrated to start dinging and flashing whenever the tank was 7/8 Full, instead of 7/8 Empty.
Our "food gauge" was designed a very long time ago to remind us to start looking for food for our next meal. Knowing that the next meal will be there gives us the "luxury" (and the responsibility) of choice.

[pause]

Lookin' For Lunch In All The Wrong Places

"In general, mankind, since the improvement of cookery, eats twice as much as nature requires."
Benjamin Franklin (1706 – 1790).

Going out for a little lunch? Maybe a little thought about lunch a little ahead of time can help.

Same thing goes for breakfast and dinner.

Many menus have "expanded" to try to include "healthier" fare, but those "healthier" items can sometimes be either Not-So-Healthier or quite a bit more McSpensive.

When it comes time to order, it's good to remember that a "square" meal doesn't mean: "excessive" or "maximum."

YOU ARE WHAT YOU ORDER.

How often do you Lunch Box it or Brown Bag it?
Think of the Possibilities!

[pause]

Late Weight

Skipping breakfast and/or lunch is probably not a healthy way to go.

Oftentimes, there's that creepy feeling of "emptiness" that comes out late at night, subconsciously calling out to you to "follow your gut" to the kitchen.

That creepy feeling is nevermore apparent than on those nights when one has "passed" on breakfast, lunch, or both.

Yep,
The
WHOLE
Enchilada.

Picture yourself with your head in the refrigerator, freezer, or cupboard late at night. Now picture yourself pondering over what led you to the kitchen. Was it a $3^2 + H_2O$ day? Maybe not.

[pause]

Me, Myself, And Ice Cream

"I doubt whether the world holds for anyone a more soul-stirring surprise than the first adventure with ice-cream."
Heywood Broun (1888 – 1939).

Ice cream is way up there on the list of foods that come to my mind if and when I can't dismiss the thought of eating.

If and when that happens, I try to redirect my thoughts to the next meal.

It will make that meal that much better - and, once in a while, there's ice cream for dessert!

LIFE IS
CHOCK-FULL
OF CHOICES.

Back to Pavlov for a minute here: What if Dr. Pavlov had chosen to be an ice cream vendor, instead of a behavioral physiologist?
Picture him in his white uniform, wearing his white hat, driving his white truck around, ringing that bell like crazy!
I'll bet he'd have been good at it.
Let's keep in mind that Lapses (both intentional and unintentional) are part of Life and can be factored into our "personalized" plans.

[pause]

Chapter 5. WEIGHING IN

a funambulist
the midnight oil
Julia
a very pleasant talk
the count
a good body
an escape artist

THE HEAVYWEIGHT FIGHT

There's an old English proverb that goes:

"Often and little eating makes a man fat."

[pause]

A Balancing Act

In 1859, Jean-Francois Gravelet ("The Great Blondin") became the
first tightrope walker (funambulist) to cross Niagara Falls.

How we got here:
We took in more calories than we burned.

Calories In > Calories Burned.

How we get back to where we want to be:
We take in fewer calories than we burn until we get there.

Calories In < Calories Burned.

What we do when we get to where we want to be:
We balance the calories taken in with the calories burned.

Calories In = Calories Burned.

How we accomplish this Balancing Act:
We apply The Theory Of Bellytivity.

$$E = 3^2 + H_2O.$$

IT'S EASY
TO LOSE LE TRACK.

Picture yourself on the balance beam at the Olympics (well, maybe at
some gym). Think of things in a typical day that throw you off balance
a little, or a lot. Keep walking – don't stop until the next meal.

[pause]

It's About Time

It's really pretty simple (at least until it gets complicated).

All you really have to measure is Time:

"The Breakfast Hour."
"The Lunch Hour."
"The Dinner Hour."

Do these sound like phrases from the past? They are!

How about: "Don't eat between meals"?

Long before we even knew what Time was (do we now?), the 24-hour cycle was essential to our survival.

Nowadays, it's still important to try to stay on that same cycle with our meals, as well as with our sleep.

HOUR
POWER.

Try to picture the old, old days.
Imagine everyone "awakening" at sunrise and "retiring" at sunset – occasionally having to "burn the midnight oil."
By eating three square meals a day, each meal at about the same time each day, people back then were pretty much forced to maintain what for us would be called a Healthy Lifestyle.

[pause]

The Joy Of Being Cooked For

"I was 32 when I started cooking. Up until then, I just ate."
Julia Child (1912 – 2004).

Wouldn't it be great to have someone in every household who would prepare everyone else's meals and remind each of them not to eat between meals – and would love doing it?

Any volunteers out there?

If not, there's gotta be a little Planning and Communication involved.

Hey, somebody's gotta figure out What, When, and Where each Next Meal is going to be – ahead of time.

FOOD
FORETHOUGHT.

Picture everyone arriving home at once, all hungry for dinner.
There's nothing prepared. What do you do?
There's always the quick fixes – maybe not so healthy and often $$$.

Now, picture all arriving home with dinner prepared ahead of time, but in the refrigerator, just needing to be warmed up. Well, HalleJulia!

[pause]

Braving The Craving

"He (Albert Einstein) *knows as much about psychology as I do about physics, so we had a very pleasant talk."*
Sigmund Freud (1856 – 1939).

A craving (formerly called psychological dependence) is a very strong desire for something (food, alcohol, drugs, cigarettes, gambling, other) that produced a pleasant psychological feeling in the past.

The dilemma with food is that we can't just totally quit eating. We have to eat enough, yet <u>not</u> <u>too</u> <u>much</u>.

What The Theory Of Bellytivity is all about is this: not only "not too much," but also "<u>Not</u> <u>Too</u> <u>Often</u>."

HABIT
YOUR
WAY.

It's called "Giving In." It starts subconsciously, but must involve some conscious awareness – often not much!
It might be tough sometimes to smile and say "No, Thank You," but always remember: It's <u>Your</u> Choice!

[pause]

Just Don't Do It

"Who's on First?"
Irving Gordon (1915 – 1996).

It's just me and the refrigerator. All alone. No referee.

I reach; I pull the door open.

I lose. No, I gain.

I win. No, I lose.

Stop!

Why did I do what I did?

Was it me or my state of subconsciousness?

It sure wasn't the refrigerator!

IT'S A
LOSE / WIN
SITUATION.

Picture yourself at the refrigerator. You've been there, haven't you? We've all been there.
On occasion, we find ourselves finding ourselves needing to explain to ourselves that, although we're hungry, we don't need any more calories until the next meal. The count is full: $3^2 + H_2O$.

[pause]

Exorcise Those Pounds Away

"I'd do anything for a good body except diet and exercise."
Steve Martin (1945 -   ).

Exercising and "Exorcising" can work together, even simultaneously.

Exercise helps us to retain muscle and to reduce fat. Wow! Even just a little exercise every day can benefit our health. You might want to choose an activity that gives you a positive feeling.

"Exorcise" helps to "expel" hunger pangs from our minds. By learning to ignore all those pangs, rather than taking in peripheral calories, we get a positive feeling, too - from having made a good choice.

Exercise can increase calories burned between meals, while "Exorcise" can decrease calories consumed between meals.

LEAN
ON ME.

Picture tipping the bathroom scales, noticing that your weight is up a couple of pounds from yesterday, then making some kind of mental note of this to yourself, such as:
"Either Go Easy On Dessert Or Walk The Dog A Few More Blocks."
That's what it comes down to:
Calories Consumed v. Calories Burned.

[*pause*]

Running Lapses

"The human capacity for guilt is such that people can always find ways to blame themselves."
Stephen Hawking (1942 -   ).

Lapses occur.

When they do, one good way to help avoid Re-Lapses is to make some sort of physical or mental gesture to show awareness and recognition:

Maybe a couple of extra minutes next time you exercise.

Maybe a quick: Who? What? When? Where? Why? hoW?

Maybe taking the farthest, rather than closest, parking spot.

NO
PORKING
BETWEEN
MEALS.

Most importantly, rather than looking back with Guilt or Blame, picture yourself trying to devise a workable plan to better avoid future lapses. You gotta think like a Scientist here, not like an Escape Artist.

[pause]

Chapter 6. ZEN AND THE ART OF METABOLIC MAINTENANCE

sound bites
an annoying friend
too serious
that lady
gravity

MIND OVER FATTER

To me, it seems that either nobody knows for sure what Zen is or that those who do know aren't telling.

Maybe Zen is simply an acceptance of one's true place in the scheme of things as a small part of some vast, beautiful work of art; but, then again, maybe not.

Let's try using Zen in a narrower sense here to stand for seeing things beyond what's been placed in front of us; seeing things as they really are, rather than as another person wants us to see them.

[pause]

Stream Of Unconsciousness

"Shut your eyes and see."
James Joyce (1882 – 1941).

There seems to be an almost-constant stream of mostly unwanted messages bombarding our senses throughout our waking hours – many pertaining to food and drink.

In their own way, Maybe Our Brains are Becoming Obese! We're taking in far too many "empty calories" of useless information than we're able to "burn."

Somehow, we need to find the mental strength to sort out and separate those unending "sound bites," "trailers," and "videos" that the beamers and streamers keep sending us - to prevent them from playing through, and with, our minds.

In many ways, it's like turning a device off and charging it. (Are we maybe becoming the "devices"?)

YOU,
YOURSELF,
AND YOU.

Picture yourself sitting in a very comfortable chair in a soundproof room with very low light, shielded from all the distractions that constantly surround you.   Can you hear me now?

[pause]

Belly And The Beast

"I keep eating for fear I will be hungry."
Mason Cooley (1927 – 2002).

Can we tame it – like a wild horse, or is it un-trainable – like my wife's husband?

If we feed it, it will go away…but we will have taken in calories that we may not need, or even want.

It raises its ugly head even more often while we're on Maintenance – when we need Bellytivity the most!

Maybe we should think of Hunger not as our enemy, but more as a kind of "annoying friend."

IS THE BEAST IN THE BELLY?
OR
IS THE BELLY IN THE BEAST?

Visualize yourself ignoring the behavior of that "annoying friend" until your next meal: maybe you'll be less likely to gain those pounds back.

[pause]

Where There's A Weigh There's A Will

"Do the best you can, and don't take life too serious."
Will Rogers (1879 – 1935).

Will power doesn't do much good "once-in-a-while."

It has to be pretty much ongoing.

In order to avoid experiencing too many backslides, someone (hey, I think that means You) must Monitor the Status of the Project.

The whole idea of Three Square Meals A Day Plus Water should work for many of us. But, for all of us, things happen.

Weighing every day is probably the best way to keep track of fluctuations.

REFRAIN
FROM
REGAIN.

Picture those Lapses piling up like a stack of pancakes.
Now, picture your face when you look down at the scales and see that you're 5 pounds above your chosen weight.
Not to panic.
Quickly, you re-Gain your composure and devise a plan to re-Lose a little weight.

[pause]

Lighten Up!

"It's not what you look at that matters. It's what you see."
Henry David Thoreau (1817 – 1862).

So, we've almost reached the end; or is it the beginning?

Whad'ya think? Can you handle it from here?

Is it Simple? Is it Do-able?

Time to go to 3^2 + H$_2$O and to enjoy Guilt-Free Eating again?

Here it is:
For 2 weeks: Strictly 3^2 + H$_2$O.
For awhile after that: Lifestyle Meets Bellytivity.
Finally: The Zen Of When.

It soon may be the end for some, or the beginning for others; but, for me, the challenge just continues to continue; and:

IT AIN'T OVER
'TIL
THAT LADY
"DIETS."

Picture finishing this book, standing in front of that familiar refrigerator door, and just smiling…as you think to yourself: "No, Thank You."

[pause]

To Market, To Market

The Words By Which We Lose,
Whichever Ones We Choose,
Should Make Us Contemplate
The Gravity Of Weight.

A Plethora of Pertinent Printed Products for Purchase
awaits you at the following websites:

www.bellytivity.com
www.thetheoryofbellytivity.com
www.lightenupdiet.com
www.3squareh2o.com

Picture yourself happy to be alive and well. And, well, anyway, as to the products above, if you think that a few contemplative words or symbols might be of benefit to you and yours, then, by all means, Help Yourself!   Thanks for reading my book.

EPILOGUE: After Words

a compass

THROUGH THICK AND THIN

I wrote this book late last millennium, in my spare time. I had a lot of fun with it. All it was was common sense, with a little humor added in.

The concept of the book is so simple that, at one point, several years ago now, it was "reduced" to an "abridged" version, just one page in width (similar to what's on the next page). It was then submitted for consideration as:

"World's Thinnest Diet Book."

A polite person at Guinness politely said in a polite manner that she was very sorry, but they had no category for "thinness of diet books."

So, I kept my tongue in my cheek, went back to the blackboard, added a little "wit," a little "wisdom," and a lotta "pictures" to the formula and "bulked" the book up to a "healthy" width.

[pause]

Words To Live And Diet By

"Water, taken in moderation, cannot hurt anybody."
Mark Twain (1835 – 1910).

TALK AND LISTEN TO YOUR DOCTOR.
Be sure that you're healthy enough to avoid calories between meals.

EAT 3 SQUARE MEALS PER DAY.
Don't skip meals. Allow up to one hour for each meal, at about the same time each day, if possible.

CONSUME ONLY WATER BETWEEN MEALS.
Modify if and when necessary and/or important.

PRACTICE BELLYTIVITY.
Situations arise. Be wise. Use responsible awareness.

EXERCISE.
Feel a positive sense of accomplishment during and after.

WEIGH EVERY DAY.
Like a compass, the scales will tell you which direction you're going.

PLAN AND PREPARE MEALS AHEAD.
Buy ahead, chop ahead, cook ahead. Utilize leftovers.

BUY HEALTHY FOOD.
We all know what's healthy, don't we?

TAKE LAPS FOR LAPSES.
Do something physical (and/or mental), such as running laps (and/or questioning the Lapse), after every Lapse.

TELL OTHERS WHAT YOU'RE DOING.
They'll understand when you smile and say: "No, Thank You."

LIGHTEN UP!
Enjoy the life you live.

[pause]

GLOSSARY

bellytivity. (n.) The responsible awareness of when (and when not) to put calories into one's own stomach. *It ain't that tough…after awhile.*

caloric entrepreneur. (n.) One who creates and/or produces and/or promotes caloric products for sale to others (for a profit). *Alias: The Candy Man.*

calorization. (n.) The act of consuming food and/or drink that contains calories.

calorize. (v.) To consume food and/or drink that contains calories.

chemicalorie. (n.) A calorie from a molecule that has been "tinkered with."

historical futurism. (n.) The science of evaluating something from the present or past by asking "what if" from a future perspective.

idle momentum. (n.) The tendency to remain idle when idle.
When Velocity = 0, then Mass x Velocity = 0.

lapse. (n.) The act of consuming calories between meals.
(v.) To consume calories between meals.

lighten up. (v.) 1. To stop taking things too seriously. 2. To lose a little weight. 3. To enlighten one's self as to one's "surroundings." 4. All of the above.

obesetacle. (n.) 1. A caloric obstacle blocking the path from one meal to the next. 2. A situation, habit, circumstance, or condition that can potentially get in one's way while one is trying to avoid the temptation of Peripheral Calories.
e.g. McFork-In-The-Road and other Fast-Food-Forks-In-The-Road.

passive activity. (n.) The observational interest one takes in the activities of others while remaining physically inactive oneself.

peripheral calories. (n.) Calories consumed during the period of time outside the breakfast, lunch, and dinner hours (between meals).

phantom calorie. (n.) A pseudocalorie disguised as a calorie.

pseudocalorie. (n.) A chemical that tastes caloric, but is not.

sales pitcher. (n.) One who uses "tactics" to try to persuade others to purchase products or services they may or may not need (for salary, commission, or profit).
Who's in Your wallet?

(the) six w's. (n.) Who? What? When? Where? Why? hoW?

square meal. (n.) A meal that is balanced, filling, healthy, nourishing, satisfying, substantial, wholesome; not maximum or excessive.   *Worth waiting for.*

(the) state of ideal weight. (n.) The initial achievement and, then, the long-term maintenance of a healthy weight by a healthy person through the practice of Bellytivity.   *A great state to live in.*

(the) theory of bellytivity ($E = 3^2 + H_2O$). (n.) The energy (E) needed by a healthy individual to achieve and maintain a healthy weight and lifestyle can be obtained from 3 square meals per day (3^2) plus water (H_2O).
                                         Brilliant. Who thought that one up?

(the) theory of square progression. (n.) The relationship of the square of any whole number (x^2) to the square of the preceding whole number $(x - 1)^2$ can be expressed in the formula $x^2 = (x - 1)^2 + 2x - 1$.   *e.g. $3^2 = (3 - 1)^2 + (2 \times 3) - 1$.*

(the) zen of when. (n.) The positive feeling of accomplishment and maintenance of a healthy weight and a healthy lifestyle through the practice of Bellytivity.
                                         Don't Worry, Be Healthy.

www.ingramcontent.com/pod-product-compliance
Lightning Source LLC
Chambersburg PA
CBHW081213020426
42331CB00012B/3022